HEINEMANN Profiles

Margaret Thatcher

An Unauthorized Biography

Sean Connolly

Heinemann Library
Chicago, Illinois

Designed by Visual Image
Originated by Dot Gradations
Printed and bound in Hong Kong/China

05 04 03 02 01
10 9 8 7 6 5 4 3 2 1

Library of Congress Cataloging-in-Publication Data
Connolly, Sean, 1956-
        Margaret Thatcher / Sean Connolly.
        p. cm. – (Heinemann profiles)
        Includes bibliographical references and index.
        Summary: Profiles the former British prime minister, with information on her
childhood, family life, career, and the legacy of her administration.
        ISBN 1-57572-224-0 (library binding)
        1. Thatcher, Margaret—Juvenile literature. 2. Prime ministers—Great
Britain—Biography—Juvenile literature. [1. Thatcher, Margaret. 2. Prime ministers. 3.
Women—Biography.] I. Title. II. Series.
DA591.T47 C65 2000
941.085'8'092—dc21
        [B]   99-089880

Acknowledgments
The Publishers would like to thank the following for permission to reproduce photographs: Camera
Press, p. 22; Hulton Getty, pp. 6, 13, 21, 27; PA News, pp. 14, 15, 17, 25, 47, 51; PA Reuter Photo, p. 11;
Rex Features, pp. 5, 7, 8, 18, 19, 20, 23, 26, 28, 30, 33, 35, 36, 37, 38, 40, 43, 44, 46, 49, 50; Frank
Spooner Pictures/P. Piel, p. 31.

Cover photograph reproduced with permission of Rex Features.

Every effort has been made to contact copyright holders of any material reproduced in this book. Any
omissions will be rectified in subsequent printings if notice is given to the publisher.

Some words are shown in bold, **like this.** You can find out what they mean by looking in the glossary.

This is an unauthorized biography. The subject has not sponsored or endorsed this book.

CONTENTS

WHO IS MARGARET THATCHER?

No U.S. president except Franklin Roosevelt has served longer than eight years, but for over a decade the United Kingdom (U.K.) knew only one **prime minister**—Margaret Thatcher. She led the country from 1979 until 1990, winning three **general elections,** and shaping British politics in a way that few other leaders have ever done. In addition to being the first woman prime minister in British history, she held power for a longer period than any other prime minister in the twentieth century.

SOLID VALUES

Margaret Thatcher learned many lessons from her father, Alfred, who taught her the importance of **thrift,** determination, and hard work. He also displayed a strong sense of pride in Britain. These were the same values that Mrs. Thatcher brought to her **Conservative** party as its leader, and later to the whole country as prime minister. She tried to

"They won't turn the clock back more than a third of the distance. They can't. She's changed the **Labour** party far more than the Conservative party."

> Alan Walters, Conservative adviser,
> talking about Mrs. Thatcher's influence on future
> Labour party governments, 1989

Margaret
Thatcher's
leadership
helped lead
the U.K. out of
an economic
recession.

reverse the decline that the British economy had seen in the 1970s, while also aiding British interests in Europe and beyond.

Few other leaders have given their names to entire sets of values and **policies,** but people around the world are familiar with the word "Thatcherism." Her leadership was so consistent and unchanging that she became known as the "Iron Lady."

OPPOSING VOICES

In the end, Thatcher's strong opinions gradually weakened her position as leader, as once-loyal **allies** felt that they no longer had a say in governing the country. Joining with her longstanding **opponents,** they delivered the blow that ended her leadership. Even so, she remains a strong presence, and her views on British life influence today's politicians.

ABOVE THE SHOP

Margaret Thatcher was born Margaret Hilda Roberts in Grantham, Lincolnshire, England, on October 13, 1925. Grantham was—and still is today—the sort of place that people describe as "Middle England." This term usually describes places where people hold traditional values, such as honesty and **thrift.**

A STRONG INFLUENCE

Margaret's family certainly held these traditional values. Her father, Alfred Roberts, was a successful grocer who had left school at thirteen to set up his own store. Through hard work and careful planning, he had built his shop into a thriving small business. Both Margaret and her sister, Muriel, were born in a room above the store. Margaret's mother, Beatrice, was content to stay at home, taking care of the two girls and managing the household.

"He [her father] taught me that you first sort out what you believe in. You then apply it. You don't **compromise** on things that matter."
Margaret Thatcher, 1979

Alfred Roberts was a leader in the local politics of Grantham. He held the post of **alderman,** and he took his responsibilities seriously. Alfred believed in leading by example, and he wanted the voters of Grantham to see that he could offer the town the same virtues that he showed in building his own business. He was proud of his town and also of being British. Addressing a dinner of Grantham business leaders in 1937, he claimed that he would rather shine shoes in Britain than be "a leading citizen in a good many of the other leading countries in the world today, because I know I can get tolerance and justice from my fellow men."

Margaret learned about the value of money by helping in Alfred Roberts's small corner shop.

Margaret agreed with such statements and continued to carry the same feelings throughout her own life. She also remembered some other advice her father gave his daughters: never hold an opinion simply because other people hold it.

SIMPLE TASTES

The Roberts family belonged to the Methodist church, which teaches the same sort of hardworking values that were so important to Alfred. The family attended church each Sunday, and Alfred tried to use his position as a local **councillor** to make sure that Sundays in Grantham were reserved for worship.

As a schoolgirl, Margaret was always neat and well-behaved.

Alfred extended his belief in simple pleasures and hard work to his family. Even as children, both girls spent hours helping out in the shop, watching as money was carefully counted and lists of expenses were entered into the shop's books. Neither girl had a bicycle, and they rarely went to the movies or the theater. They were not denied these things because the family was poor; it was simply that Alfred felt that these

pleasures were not worth the money they cost. In the
same way, the Roberts family rarely had hot baths, since
Alfred saved money by not having a hot water system
in the house.

SUCCESS AT SCHOOL

Alfred believed in the value of education, and he was
proud when Margaret won a scholarship to Kesteven
and Grantham Girls' School, the best school in the area.
Margaret was a disciplined child and worked hard at her
studies. Her schoolbag always bulged with books, and
she was never shy about asking questions in class. Her
school reports showed that she was well-behaved and
ambitious, and several teachers predicted that she would
be a great success in the future.

Although Margaret's qualities at school were hard work
and discipline, rather than natural brilliance, she did
have a special talent in
one field—debating.
Margaret was not afraid
to ask difficult questions,
and she answered any
questions she was asked
with great calm and
self-confidence. These
skills were very helpful
in her later life.

"I don't think she
[Margaret] has much
of a sense of humor, I
don't think her father
had, and I certainly
don't think her
mother had."
    Margaret Wickstead,
    a childhood friend,
        1986

THE OUTSIDE WORLD

Kesteven and Grantham Girls' School was proud of the fact that several girls passed the exams each year to enter either Oxford or Cambridge University. Margaret was determined to be one of them when her turn came, and her father backed her all the way. She had concentrated on chemistry in her last years at school, so she had to take lessons in Latin and review other subjects in order to prepare for these important exams. After many late nights of studying, Margaret passed her exams and was put onto a waiting list. In 1943, she was offered a place at Somerville College, Oxford, to study chemistry.

AN EXCITING NEW LIFE

Except for a week spent in London, Margaret had never really been away from Grantham. Oxford was like another world to her, with its ancient buildings, learned professors, and students who came from very rich backgrounds. Most students, unlike Margaret, came from **public schools,** and had an easy confidence about everything they did. These students were also more experienced than Margaret was in dealing with people who served them, such as the college **porters** and cleaners.

Margaret, however, retained her common sense and did not let herself get discouraged by her new

Oxford's ancient buildings and centuries-old traditions were very different from familiar Grantham.

surroundings. As always, work came first, and at an **elite** university such as Oxford, the work was hard. Students who could not keep up risked being expelled. Margaret never ran that risk. Just as she had done in previous years, she let her hard work and discipline overcome her lack of natural brilliance.

UNIVERSITY POLITICS

Margaret became interested in politics as soon as she entered Oxford. Universities are always good places to hear heated political debates, and Margaret found herself swept up in them immediately. Her views had been shaped by her father's strong opinions on the importance of careful management of money. These views were echoed by the **Conservative** party, and Margaret chose to join the Oxford University Conservative Association (OUCA) in her first year.

The OUCA was mainly a social club when Margaret joined, although members sometimes made speeches in the surrounding towns and villages. OUCA members also helped in the war effort, since the Second World War was raging. They collected goods that could be used by the military and helped maintain defenses in the area.

The 1945 **general election** gave Margaret a taste of national politics. She attended meetings in support of the **Conservative candidate** for Oxford. Margaret also returned to Grantham during the election, to

Party politics

Throughout most of the twentieth century, the United Kingdom has been governed by one of two political parties—the Conservative party or the **Labour** party. Each of these parties stands for a set of values, and voters choose between the parties and their overall values at each election. One major difference between the parties is the way in which they handle government money. The Labour party has tried to improve conditions of the poor and needy by using tax money to help these groups. Tax money also goes to give **unemployed** people an income until they can find another job. The Conservatives, on the other hand, believe that by reducing taxes, people will have a chance to keep more of their earnings. With less tax to pay, they argue, people will be encouraged to take risks and set up their own companies. These new companies will in turn create more jobs and help unemployed people in that way.

speak out against a candidate there. Denis Kendall, the member of **Parliament** (M.P.) from Grantham, had first been elected in 1942, and three years later was trying to persuade voters to vote against the Conservatives. Margaret spoke to women's groups in an effort to build support for the Conservatives. Back at Oxford, she led moves to make the OUCA more active, and in her last year she was elected president of the organization.

Denis Kendall, the Grantham M.P., was an independent candidate who was elected without the support of a political party.

PUTTING LEARNING INTO PRACTICE

After receiving her degree in 1945, Margaret knew that she had to put her learning to good use. It was time to stand on her own two feet, as her father might have said. Her first job was doing chemical research for a plastics company in Essex. After working there for four years, Margaret found a job testing the quality of cake fillings and ice cream for the Lyons Company in London. Despite her satisfaction with this work, Margaret still had the taste for something else—politics. She had made political connections while working in Essex, so she continued to live there, even though her work was now in London.

FIRST POLITICAL STEPS

Margaret had thoroughly enjoyed her experience with politics while at Oxford, and she began to think of ways in which she could build a political career. In 1946, **Parliament** voted for a pay raise for M.P.s. The new annual salary was only about $1,600—about $56,000 in today's money—but it was enough to live on. Margaret had been worried that a career in politics would not pay well, but now her concerns evaporated. In her spare time, she began studying law, since a good knowledge of the law would be important in politics.

AN EXPECTED SETBACK

Margaret became involved in **Conservative** associations in Essex and attended the annual Conservative party conferences. She set her sights on becoming a **candidate** in the **general election** that was going to take place in 1950. Although only twenty-four years old, she was chosen as the Conservative candidate for Dartford, Kent. The **Labour** candidate was expected to win this **constituency,** but the party officials thought that Margaret might learn from her experience.

Conservative candidate Margaret Roberts met with the chairman of the Conservative party, Lord Woolton, in 1951.

Margaret lost the election, as expected, but voters and Conservative officials were impressed with her thoroughness and persistence. The pattern was repeated the following year, as the Labour party again won the Dartford seat. But Margaret's political skills and her youth—she was the youngest woman candidate in both elections—ensured that she would not be forgotten.

Newlyweds Denis and Margaret Thatcher were an ideal match for each other.

PARTNER FOR LIFE

Margaret had met a young businessman named Denis Thatcher during her first Dartford **campaign**. The Thatcher family had a successful chemical company in Kent, and Denis ran it skillfully. He had been married before the war, but divorced soon afterward, and wanted to marry again. The two admired each other, fell in love, and married in December 1951.

The new man in Margaret's life shared many of Alfred Roberts's views. There was one important difference, though. Unlike Alfred, Denis believed that women should have the chance to explore their chosen careers.

"In this way, gifts and talents that would otherwise be wasted are developed to the benefit of the community."
Margaret Thatcher, writing about women pursuing careers, 1952

M.P. FOR FINCHLEY

B y marrying someone as wealthy as Denis, Margaret was free to consider politics without any worries about the low salary. She was able to leave her job and continue to study law. Margaret passed her **bar exams** in 1953. That same year, she gave birth to twins, Mark and Carol. She stayed home with the babies for a while, but the Thatchers soon hired a live-in nanny so that Margaret could pursue her goals in law and politics.

Still, despite the advantages she seemed to have, Margaret faced an uphill battle in her early political career. Although Denis supported the idea of female careers, it seemed as though the voters—or at least the party officials who chose **candidates**—thought otherwise. Of the 625 M.P.s in the early 1950s, only seventeen were women.

TRYING FOR A SEAT

Margaret spent the mid-1950s practicing law and taking care of her two young children. At the same time, she was on the lookout for a **constituency** where she might become the **Conservative** candidate. She was turned down for several during this time, but in 1958, she was accepted for the north London suburb of Finchley. The choice was ideal—it was close to home as well as to

Margaret Thatcher's twin children, Carol and Mark, grew up in an atmosphere of success and high achievement.

Parliament itself. Most importantly, it was "winnable"—at the last election, the Conservative candidate had gained a **majority** of 12,000 votes.

Margaret rose to the challenge, **campaigning** brilliantly and speaking on a wide range of national and international subjects. When the votes were counted in the 1959 election, she had not only won, but had increased the majority to 16,260 votes. It was time to enter Parliament.

"Should a woman arise equal to the task, I say let her have an equal chance with the men for the leading **cabinet** posts. Why not a woman **chancellor**? Or **foreign secretary?**"

Margaret Thatcher, 1952

The 1959 election was a triumph not only for Margaret Thatcher, but also for the **Conservative** party itself. Under the leadership of Harold Macmillan, the Conservatives returned to power for a third straight **term,** with a **majority** of 100 seats in the **House of Commons**. Macmillan was a popular leader, and British people felt comfortable with him as **prime minister.** They seemed to echo a comment Macmillan had made in 1957: "Most of our people have never had it so good."

Britain regained much of its prosperity under the leadership of Prime Minister Harold Macmillan.

GAINING NOTICE

Margaret was ambitious, and showed from the beginning that she was unlikely to settle for being a **backbencher.** An M.P.'s first **parliamentary** speech is known as his or her maiden speech, and is usually short and a bit dull—simply a way of getting over stage fright. Margaret, however, spoke without notes for twenty-seven minutes. Fellow Conservatives, and even some **Labour** M.P.s, congratulated her on her skillful performance.

Margaret had spoken in favor of a **bill** to allow the press to attend public meetings freely. It was not an earth-shattering bill, but it passed through the Commons and was approved. Margaret also showed herself to be well-informed about taxes. The Conservative parliamentary officials recognized a rising star in their ranks and offered her the job of parliamentary secretary at the ministry of pensions, which she naturally accepted. Such a position is usually seen as the first rung in the ladder that leads to higher offices in government, and Margaret's case would prove to be no exception.

The political atmosphere of the 1960s was very heated. Many M.P.s, such as Enoch Powell, stirred the passions of voters with their extreme views.

THE FRINGES OF POWER

Margaret was able to put her skills and training to good use in her new post. It took someone with great concentration and an eye for detail to read all the documents involved with the job. Margaret performed this role well, even though her duties kept her from the real political action, such as major decisions about the economy and foreign affairs.

INTO GOVERNMENT

I n the end, Margaret's job as **parliamentary** secretary lasted only two years. In 1963, **Prime Minister** Macmillan resigned because of ill health. Lord Home, who took over as prime minister, narrowly lost the **general election** in 1964, as Harold Wilson led the **Labour** party to power with a **majority** of only four seats.

A DEVELOPING ROLE

After the 1964 defeat, the **Conservatives** dropped Lord Home as party leader, and replaced him with Edward Heath. Labour's majority in the **House of Commons** was slim, but after the 1966 election, it increased to 97. Margaret Thatcher was eager to join the ranks of her party leaders in their attacks on the Labour government.

Her chance came in October 1967, when she was appointed to a minor position in the **shadow**

Prime Minister Edward Heath (seated, center) was a powerful political figure who would later become one of Thatcher's critics.

cabinet. A year later, she became shadow minister for education. By now, even the most old-fashioned Conservative party leaders agreed that it was important to have at least one woman in the shadow cabinet. No other Conservative woman M.P. was as experienced as Margaret Thatcher, so her position in the party's leadership now seemed secure.

CABINET MEMBER

Prime Minister Harold Wilson called a general election in June 1970. The Labour party, **opinion polls,** and most of the public expected that Wilson would be returned for another **term** as prime minister. However, the shadow cabinet and other senior Conservatives rallied behind their leader in a successful **campaign**, and to everyone's surprise, Edward Heath became prime minister.

Margaret visited many schools as part of her role as shadow minister for education in the 1960s.

The 1960s had brought about many changes, including the idea that women can and should pursue their own careers. The reasoning that helped Margaret Thatcher enter the shadow cabinet—that there should be at least one woman in it—was carried through to the **cabinet** itself. Margaret Thatcher became the secretary of state for education and science.

PARTY LEADER

M argaret Thatcher still wanted more than a senior government position. Always looking ahead, she felt that she would spend perhaps two years in the post before being moved up the ladder to a more important position.

A STUBBORN LEADER

At first, **Prime Minister** Heath regarded the only female member of his **cabinet** very highly. He admired Thatcher's ability to get hold of an idea and stay with it. Heath himself had been elected with promises of making sweeping changes to the country. In Margaret Thatcher, he believed he had a like-minded **ally**.

Gradually, however, things began to change. Heath began to get tired of Thatcher's stubbornness, and he came to believe that she would not listen carefully enough before making up her mind. In many ways, Heath's change of view reflected a personal opinion, as if he had begun to dislike her as a person.

Many businesses had to operate in semi-darkness during a miners' strike in 1973.

ELECTION SETBACK

Even if she had fallen out of favor with the prime minister, Thatcher did become friendly with another cabinet member, Keith Joseph. The two were close during the hectic events of 1974. First, in February, the **Conservatives** lost power in a closely fought **general election,** but Heath remained the party leader. Meanwhile, Keith Joseph began making public statements about how the Conservatives had lost their way, using his Center for **Policy** Studies as a **mouthpiece**.

Keith Joseph's blunder in a public speech opened the door for Mrs. Thatcher's bid to be Conservative party leader.

The Conservatives lost another general election on October 10, 1974, and still Edward Heath refused to resign. Several senior Conservatives thought about trying for leadership of the party. Joseph announced his intention to be leader, but had to abandon his plans when he made an embarrassing speech that seemed to say that poor people should not be allowed to have children. His dropping out meant that Thatcher was free to try. She announced her plans in early 1975. Like Joseph, she argued that the Conservatives under Heath had not been conservative enough about spending. She had many powerful allies, including the war hero Airey Neave.

Closing In

Conservative M.P.s voted in a leadership election on February 4, 1975. In the first ballot, Thatcher got more votes than Heath, who then resigned. A week later, there was a second ballot. This time around, more **candidates** entered, several of whom agreed with Heath's way of leading and had not wanted to run directly against him in the first ballot. This second ballot was decisive: Margaret Thatcher got nearly twice as many votes as her nearest rival, William Whitelaw. She was the new party leader.

That vote proved to be a turning point in British politics. It opened up many possibilities for other women, since a woman was now the leader of one of the major political parties. For Thatcher, the next step was, of course, to cap this achievement by becoming **prime minister.** But first, there was the small matter of defeating the **Labour** government. However, that prospect did not worry her, and she started planning party strategy from the day she took over as leader.

"To me it is like a dream that the next name on the list after Macmillan, Sir Alec Douglas-Home, and Edward Heath is Margaret Thatcher."

Margaret Thatcher, after being elected leader of the Conservative party, 1975

Thatcher relished the chance to attack the Labour government during the 1979 election.

LABOUR ISN'T WORKING

Margaret Thatcher's new title was leader of the **Opposition**. She appointed people to her **shadow cabinet,** with the help of the two men who had done so much in her leadership **campaign**: Keith Joseph and Airey Neave. Joseph helped her make sure that the shadow cabinet was firm about government spending. Neave, who was more of a political fighter, ensured that Thatcher included some tough fighters on her team.

The Labour government at the time was led by James Callaghan. By 1978, Labour **policies** were beginning to look poorly planned, and during the winter of 1978–79, many public-sector employees went on **strike**. The newspapers referred to this period as the "Winter of Discontent," using a phrase from the Shakespeare play *Richard III*. For the Conservatives, however, the disruption was good news. They attacked Labour for being a weak government and also for making people lose their jobs. A **general election** was called for May 1979. The Conservatives were ready with their campaign slogan: "Labour isn't working."

PRIME MINISTER THATCHER

The **Labour** government of James Callaghan was weak in several ways. In addition to the **strikes** and **union** disputes, people worried about the British **currency.** Margaret Thatcher and her **Conservative** team attacked on all these fronts, pouring scorn on the government, both in **Parliament** and in **campaign** speeches to voters.

ACHIEVING A GOAL

The Conservatives began to spell out how things would be different if they won the next **general election** and Margaret Thatcher became **prime minister.** They promised strong and decisive government, with firm action taken to control unions and to keep government spending—and

A number of strikes in early 1979 weakened the Labour government just before the election.

"The question you will have to consider is whether we risk tearing everything up by the roots."
Prime Minister James Callaghan, referring to Conservative plans in the 1979 election

taxes—as low as possible. They also hinted at one of the **policies** that would become so closely linked with the name of Margaret Thatcher—**privatization.** The Conservatives intended to begin by selling the National Freight Corporation, which at the time was owned by the state, to the public.

The combination of Thatcher's style, the poor performance of the Labour government, and Conservative election statements proved to be decisive. On the night of May 3, 1979, as general election votes were counted in each **constituency**, it became clear that Labour was losing ground. The final count showed that the Conservatives would be forming the new government, with a majority of 43 in the **House of Commons**. And leading the party—and the government—would be Britain's first woman prime minister, Margaret Thatcher.

A jubilant Margaret Thatcher, with husband Denis by her side, acknowledged the cheers after her 1979 election victory.

THE IRON LADY

The **Conservatives** had won the election largely because voters felt that **Labour** was weak in its handling of the British economy. The Conservatives promised firmer leadership in this area. But Margaret Thatcher would also show that she could be equally forceful in international matters. In the late 1970s, the **Cold War** was still going on, and Thatcher believed that the U.K. and its **allies** in **NATO,** such as the United States, should stand firm against the **Soviet Union** and its allies.

Thatcher's stance had earned her the nickname the "Iron Lady" even before she became **prime minister,** and now it was used more often. She showed her strength when Iranian **terrorists** held nineteen people **hostage** in the Iranian embassy in London. Thatcher ordered a Special Air Service (SAS) team to storm the embassy. After a dramatic battle, during which four of the five gunmen were killed, the SAS rescued all of the hostages.

THE FALKLANDS CAMPAIGN

Another international event dominated Thatcher's first **term**—the Falklands conflict. The Falkland Islands are British lands lying in the South Atlantic Ocean, near the southern tip of South America. For many years, Argentina had claimed to own the islands, and on April 2, 1982, Argentine troops invaded and captured the islands. The action was immediately **condemned,** not just by Britain, but by the **United Nations** as well.

Thatcher reacted swiftly and with determination. Within three days, a huge **task force** set off on the 8,000-mile (13,000-kilometer) journey to recapture the islands and to reclaim British **sovereignty**. The United States, led by President Ronald Reagan–who admired Thatcher—tried in vain to use **diplomacy** to avoid an all-out war.

After several naval clashes near the islands, the British forces landed on the Falklands on May 21. After two weeks of heavy fighting, they made their way to the capital, Port Stanley, where they finally overcame the Argentine forces. Argentina surrendered on June 14. The world saw this as a victory not only for Britain, but for Thatcher herself.

"Failure? The possibility does not exist."
Margaret Thatcher, referring to the Falklands campaign, April 1982

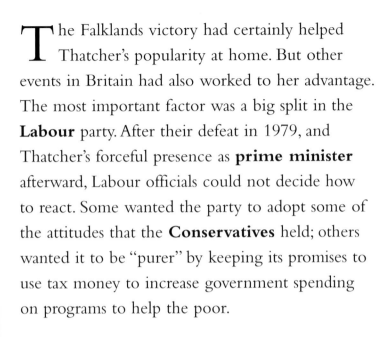

A SECOND TRIUMPH

T he Falklands victory had certainly helped
Thatcher's popularity at home. But other
events in Britain had also worked to her advantage.
The most important factor was a big split in the
Labour party. After their defeat in 1979, and
Thatcher's forceful presence as **prime minister**
afterward, Labour officials could not decide how
to react. Some wanted the party to adopt some of
the attitudes that the **Conservatives** held; others
wanted it to be "purer" by keeping its promises to
use tax money to increase government spending
on programs to help the poor.

DIVIDED OPPOSITION

In 1980, the Labour party chose Michael Foot
to replace James Callaghan as leader. Foot was
a respected politician who came from the
"purer" wing of the party. Thatcher was
pleased with this change, since she felt that
Foot represented outdated opinions that were
out of touch with the voters. Others, including
many in the Labour party, agreed. In 1981,
four leading Labour M.P.s—Roy Jenkins,
Shirley Williams, David Owen, and William
Rodgers—left the Labour party to form a new
party. The new Social **Democratic** party then
formed an alliance with the Liberal party, which

had been a weak party since the end of the First World War. Their goal was to break the two-party system of either Labour or Conservative government. However, the immediate effect was to divide those who opposed Thatcher's Conservative party.

THE FALKLANDS FACTOR

Thatcher was satisfied with the British political scene after all of these events, and called for a **general election** to be held on June 9, 1983. The **Opposition** members, now divided, spent much of their time arguing among themselves and offering confused messages to voters. Thatcher, on the other hand, presented herself as a strong leader and very much the "Iron Lady." Her success in the Falklands played a huge part in the election—this advantage was known as the Falklands Factor.

Thatcher sat in a tank in 1983 during a triumphant visit to the Falklands after their recapture.

The **Conservatives** won the election in the largest landslide since **Labour's** victory in 1945. They won an overwhelming **majority** of 144 seats, which meant that nearly every **bill** recommended by Thatcher and her team would become law.

TAKING ON THE MINERS

The morning of June 10, 1983, was business as usual for Margaret Thatcher as she looked ahead to a new **term** of office. With such a weak opposition in **Parliament,** she knew that many of the plans that had simply been ideas in her first term could now be put into action. Chief among these was a way of controlling the power of the **unions**.

Most people agreed that the unions had become too powerful. With their power to **strike,** they could cripple the country and weaken the government. Edward Heath's defeat in 1974 had been caused largely by a strike in the mining industry. Thatcher wanted new laws that would limit the power of unions to call strikes. She also knew that the loudest voice against these laws would be the powerful National Union of Mineworkers (NUM), led by Arthur Scargill.

The coal industry was run by a government-owned company known as the National Coal Board. Under Thatcher's advice, the company began to close

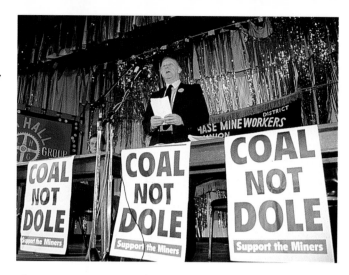

Miners' leader Arthur Scargill defied Thatcher during the bitter miners' strike that started in 1984. Thatcher's battle with the NUM had a devastating effect on many communities in Britain's coal-mining areas.

mines that were not producing enough coal. The union's reaction was swift and fierce. In March 1984, Arthur Scargill called a national miners' strike. This action soon turned violent, as striking miners attacked those who crossed **picket lines**. Thousands of police officers were moved around the country to control the outbursts. At one point, Arthur Scargill was arrested for promoting violence.

Throughout the long strike, miners lost money, and families were divided as some members went back to work. To Thatcher, Arthur Scargill had been a symbol of everything she opposed. She was tremendously pleased when the NUM finally ended the strike and returned to work on March 5, 1985.

"We had to fight an enemy without in the Falklands. We always have to be aware of the enemy within, which is more difficult to fight and more dangerous to liberty."
Margaret Thatcher, during the miners' strike, 1984

ESCAPE FROM DEATH

M argaret Thatcher and the rest of the country knew that the miners would eventually lose their battle with the government. By mid–1984, many miners were already returning to work. By the time the **Conservatives** were preparing for their annual conference in October, Thatcher sensed that victory lay ahead. Nevertheless, the mood in the country was tense. Thatcher accused the new **Labour** leader, Neil Kinnock, of aiding the NUM in its **strike** and **allying** the party to the "wreckers against the workers."

A TERRIBLE SHOCK

It was in this fighting mood that Thatcher arrived in Brighton for the Conservative conference. Then something terrible and unexpected happened. A bomb exploded in the Grand Hotel, where Thatcher and many senior Conservatives were staying. Thatcher escaped without injury, but five people were killed, and two of her leading **cabinet** members, Norman Tebbit and John Wakeham, were injured.

"This was a day I wasn't meant to see."
Margaret Thatcher, observing a fine autumn day after the Brighton bombing

The bomb had been planted by the **Irish Republican Army (IRA),** and Thatcher had been its intended victim. Television viewers around the world saw the horrific images of the dead and wounded being removed from the rubble. In the middle of it all, Thatcher walked steadily towards the assembled TV cameras. Showing no signs of fright, she said calmly, "It was an attempt not only to disrupt and terminate our conference. It was an attempt to cripple Her Majesty's **democratically** elected government."

RENEWED DETERMINATION

Margaret Thatcher's personal experience of **terrorist** violence strengthened her resolve to set an example for other terrorist organizations around the world. Notably, she refused to meet members of the African National Congress (ANC) of South Africa. The ANC leader, Nelson Mandela, had been imprisoned since 1962 for leading the struggle against the unfair **apartheid** laws in his country. In Thatcher's view, however, giving support to the pleas for his release would be like helping the IRA in her own country.

The IRA bomb destroyed a large portion of the Grand Hotel in Brighton in 1984.

THE NEW ECONOMY

Thatcher's defeat of the miners was the largest of several battles with the **unions** during her first **terms** as **prime minister**. The disputes themselves arose in large part because of the **legislation** that the **Conservatives** had put in place. The most important piece of legislation was the Employment Act, in 1982. This called for many limits to be placed on unions. In particular it attacked the idea of the closed shop, in which all the workers of a particular company must be members of a certain union. The Employment Act protected those who suffered under the closed-shop system, but it also gave employers greater freedom to fire workers who took part in a **strike.** The right of workers to strike was also limited, and union members would have to vote for strike action before it could take place.

Many people applied to buy shares in British Telecom (BT) when it was privatized.

THATCHERISM

Labor law, as this legislation was called, was only one part of the economic strategy planned by the Conservative government. Thatcher had always felt that people should be able to stand on their own two feet without government interference. She also believed that the public would become more **prosperous** if more people owned **shares** in companies.

Lord King, one of Thatcher's political **allies,** became chairman of British Airways when the company was privatized in 1987.

Added to this wish for increased share ownership was Thatcher's belief that the government should not control the large companies that provided services for the whole country (such as telephone, energy, and travel). If these companies had to compete with other companies instead of relying on handouts of government money, they could become more efficient and successful.

The Conservatives combined these two goals in a process known as privatization. Companies owned by the government were sold to private buyers, and the public could then buy shares in them. Huge government companies such as British Telecom, British Gas, and British Airways were sold off in this way. Privatization, coupled with tough labor legislation, became known as Thatcherism.

A THIRD VICTORY

PRIME MINISTER · BERNARD INGHAM

In December 1984, Thatcher invited a dynamic **Soviet** politician named Mikhail Gorbachev to Britain. Although this was still the era of the **Cold War,** she sensed that he was a new type of Soviet official, one who might be more prepared to listen to opposing views and to **compromise**. Gorbachev was impressed by what he saw in Britain: **prosperous** country villages, supermarkets full of things to buy, and highly respected scientific centers. It was obvious to Gorbachev that his own country could not match these elements of British life, and he was prepared to say so. He also seemed ready to listen to other people's opinions—something else that set him apart from other Soviet politicians.

INTERNATIONAL GO-BETWEEN

The Gorbachev visit proved to be extremely important for Thatcher. Within three months of the visit, Gorbachev became the new leader of the **Soviet Union.** He had formed a bond that bordered on friendship with Thatcher, and even sent her a warm-hearted message on her sixtieth birthday in October 1985. Thatcher was also friendly with U.S. President Ronald Reagan, leader of the world's other **superpower.** Reagan was a popular president, but he lacked the searching intelligence that Gorbachev had shown on his British visit. To President Reagan, any Soviet leader would be impossible to understand. Thatcher, on the other hand, found herself able to deal with both leaders, and sometimes paved the way for better understanding between them.

THE COUNTRY DECIDES

No matter how successful political leaders are in managing international matters, the public usually judges them on how the government has affected their daily lives. In this area, Thatcher felt confident, because the British economy was strong. **Inflation**, which had been a severe problem in the 1970s, was under control.

"I like Mr. Gorbachev; I can do business with him."
Mrs. Thatcher, at the end of Gorbachev's 1984 visit to Britain

Workers' average earnings had continued to rise since the 1983 election. Most importantly, the government was on its way to keeping its promise of lowering taxes.

By 1986, everyone knew that there would be another election soon, probably midway through 1987. Both sides were confident about victory. The **Conservatives** had a strong record of economic achievements, as well as Thatcher's image as a strong leader both at home and in international matters. On the other side, the **Opposition**—both the **Labour** party and the SDP-Liberal alliance—felt that continued **unemployment** and arguments about spending within the Conservative party itself would help them. Labour also felt that its leader, Neil Kinnock, would appeal to the young.

Rupert Murdoch, owner of many newspapers, provided loyal support for Mrs. Thatcher's election campaigns.

In the end, the election came in June 1987. The campaign had been bitter all along, but the final vote showed that Thatcher and her party had won. The Conservatives returned to power with a **majority** of 102—proof that the country still agreed with Thatcherism, or perhaps that it was still worried about Labour.

A rare defeat

In December 1984, the ruling body of Oxford University decided to award an **honorary degree** to Margaret Thatcher. Many people felt that there was nothing unusual about this idea, since several of the previous **prime ministers**—including Macmillan, Heath, and Wilson—had been awarded similar degrees. However, many teachers at the university protested. They argued that Thatcher and her government had done very little to help education in Britain. Those who were against the degree argued that the government had not given enough money to all forms of learning—from grade schools to scientists who needed money to continue their research. Many leading scientists, they said, had had to leave the country in order to find funding. Thatcher's supporters were disgusted by the protests, and were even more disgusted in January 1985, when the Oxford teachers voted 738 to 319 not to award the degree. It was Thatcher's first defeat since she lost the Dartford vote in the 1951 **general election.** She reacted with dignity, but felt hurt, and the experience left her more eager to prove the protesters wrong by winning another general election.

STORM CLOUDS

There is no doubt that the result of the 1987 **general election** was a triumph for Margaret Thatcher and her **Conservative** government. Their **majority** had been reduced, but remained high enough to push laws easily through **Parliament**. Despite their sense of joy and relief, though, some Conservatives were beginning to feel uneasy. One reason for this feeling was the very fact that they had won yet another election. Some Conservatives felt that life had become too easy for their party, and that an occasional defeat would force them to look at new ideas. Others, like former **prime minister** Heath, seemed to be holding personal grudges against Thatcher and her unwavering attitudes. Conservatives who felt that Thatcherism relied too heavily on cutting costs were called "wets." Now their voices were added to the internal debate.

"Europe will be stronger precisely because it has France as France, Spain as Spain, Britain as Britain, each with its own customs, traditions, and identity. It would be folly to try to fit them into some sort of identikit European personality."
Thatcher, part of her famous Bruges speech, 1988

DEALING WITH EUROPE

Nowhere were the disputes within the Conservative party more public than on the subject of Europe. Many of the Conservative "wets" agreed with members of the **Opposition** that Thatcher did not present a good image

Thatcher, seen here with fellow EC political leaders, faced opposition over her views on European cooperation.

of Britain within Europe as a whole. As a leading member of the **European Community (EC),** Britain was expected to play a role in lessening the differences among European countries. By reducing these differences and increasing cooperation among the nations, the EC could play a larger part in building trade within Europe.

Thatcher, on the other hand, seemed to have an "us against them" attitude towards Europe. She fought hard to protect Britain's interests, sometimes being the only European leader to reject EC proposals. Although some British people supported her efforts to reduce the amount that Britain had to pay to the EC, others felt that she was too negative. Thatcher opposed every effort to build a **federal** Europe, since she felt it would weaken Britain's **sovereignty.** She clearly outlined her views in a speech she made in the Belgian city of Bruges in September 1988.

Removed from Office

The whole issue of European union became quite complicated, and the divisions it caused within the **Conservative** party continued to grow. One particular aspect of the Conservatives' approach to the problem attracted much public attention, as well as a good deal of criticism. This area involved two elements that Thatcher felt very strongly about—money and British **sovereignty.**

The problem came to a head in 1989 with the discussion about what was known as the Exchange Rate Mechanism (ERM). The ERM was a system designed to tie European **currencies** together so that no single currency would become too strong or too weak. Many senior Conservatives, including the **chancellor of the exchequer,** Nigel Lawson, believed that Britain would gain by accepting the ERM. Thatcher, however, resisted any moves to limit

Violent demonstrations, even in some Conservative strongholds, typified the public's angry response to the poll tax.

Britain's freedom to control its own currency, the pound sterling. Eventually, on October 26, 1989, Nigel Lawson resigned from office.

THE POLL TAX

At around the same time, there was an equally difficult problem at home. It centered on a type of local tax, officially called the community charge, but informally known as the poll tax. For years, many Conservatives had felt that the rates system—the system of taxes used to pay for local services—was unfair. Under this system, which is similar to the system used in the United States, people paid local taxes according to the value of their houses. A person living in an expensive house would pay much more than the owner of a small apartment. **Tenants** would not pay any rates at all. This seemed unfair, because all of these people enjoyed the same services, such as trash collection, street repairs, and so on.

The Conservatives had thought of a new style of taxation, which they included in the 1987 election **manifesto**. Called the community charge, the system would impose exactly the same local tax on each adult individual. At first, this seemed to promise a fairer system. Soon after the election, however, complaints grew. Many people reacted angrily to the idea of a system that would let the very rich pay no more than the very poor.

A BAD COMBINATION

Poll tax protests increased in the years after the 1987 election. The **Conservatives** planned to introduce the tax in Scotland first, and then expand it to the rest of the U.K. Many Conservatives began to worry about people's angry reactions, and they tried to distance themselves from the policy. Michael Heseltine, who had held **cabinet** positions in the first Thatcher governments, was one of the most forceful critics of the poll tax.

Geoffrey Howe's dramatic resignation speech in November 1990 signaled the beginning of the end for Margaret Thatcher's reign as prime minister.

By 1990, the Conservatives had begun to look weak and divided on both the poll tax and the issues surrounding the ERM and Europe in general. The new tax was introduced in England and Wales in April 1990, and the Conservatives lost many votes in the local elections held that May. Poll tax protests reached dramatic heights, with riots and disruptions in London and elsewhere. Behind the scenes, Heseltine was meeting with many Conservative M.P.s, and it was an open secret that he was waiting for a chance to take Thatcher's place as party leader and **prime minister.**

THE FINAL BLOW

Geoffrey Howe had been **foreign secretary** for many years, but his views on Europe had differed from Thatcher's. She removed him from that position in July 1989, but kept him in the **cabinet.** Howe was insulted by her actions, and came to believe that Mrs. Thatcher had long since lost the ability to listen to people. On November 1, 1990, he resigned from the cabinet by making a dramatic speech in **Parliament**. With such divisions opening up at the highest levels, the Conservative party decided to take a leadership vote among its M.P.s. This vote would either confirm Mrs. Thatcher as leader—and prime minister—or it would replace her with a new leader.

Within days, an election was held among Conservative M.P.s. Heseltine declared himself a **candidate**. In the first round of voting, Mrs. Thatcher received more votes than Heseltine, but not enough to avoid a second round. The result showed that too many M.P.s had lost confidence in her, and Mrs. Thatcher knew that she should step down. She gave her resignation as prime minister on November 22, 1990, and left office on November 28.

Denis Thatcher, loyal as ever, watched as his wife stepped down from office on November 28, 1990.

LADY THATCHER

Margaret Thatcher had waited six days before leaving office so that the party would have a chance to elect a new leader. She drew some relief from the fact that her favorite to succeed her, John Major, won the vote on November 27. Major became the new **Conservative** leader and **prime minister** when Mrs. Thatcher stepped down.

AMONG THE LORDS

As prime minister, one of John Major's first acts was to **ennoble** Margaret Thatcher. She became Lady Thatcher of Kesteven in June 1991. With this new title, she left the **House of Commons** to begin her new role in the **House of Lords**, which is the upper house of **Parliament**. Lady Thatcher often attends sessions of the House of Lords, and her speeches still draw the attention of journalists and the public. She is still able to communicate her views on British life and on international matters.

"I waved and got into the car with Denis beside me, as he always has been; and the car took us past press, policemen and the tall black gates of Downing Street . . . out to whatever the future held."

Margaret Thatcher, describing her departure as prime minister, in *The Downing Street Years*

Foreign popularity

Thatcher enjoyed a good relationship with U.S. President Reagan and with Americans in general. Since her resignation, she has been invited by many groups—especially in the United States—to make speeches or to accept awards.

Broader interests

Being removed from the hustle and bustle of daily political life has allowed Lady Thatcher to pursue other interests. In 1993, she published her political **memoirs**, which provided a fascinating glimpse at life behind the scenes during her leadership. Lady Thatcher has also had more time to devote to travel and to her family, including her grandchildren. And her husband Denis, who had been the subject of much good-natured teasing while Margaret was prime minister, is free to play more of his beloved golf in the company of family and friends.

Judging a Career

Although leader of the **Labour** party, **Prime Minister** Tony Blair respects many of Thatcher's accomplishments.

Margaret Thatcher is the type of leader who inspires strong feelings. The values that she represented, especially her strong sense of national pride and the determined pursuit of the economic **policies** now known as Thatcherism, are ones people tend to heartily agree with or disagree with. But whatever their views, many people respect the woman who stood so firmly for what she believed to be right.

International appeal

There is an interesting parallel between Margaret Thatcher and Mikhail Gorbachev, the **Soviet** leader she so respected in the late 1980s. Both have long since lost their powerful political roles, but nonetheless remain widely respected away from their own countries. Foreigners see only the obvious benefits of what these leaders achieved, such as material wealth for some people. Many within their own countries, however, believe that this wealth has come at a terrible cost, and that they are still paying for the social divisions produced by these leaders.

BRITISH ACKNOWLEDGEMENT

Many observers have noticed the Thatcher influence on the Labour government of Tony Blair, even though the Labour party fought so hard against Thatcherism. Blair's tough position during the Kosovo crisis in 1999, coupled with his government's urging that people be encouraged to stand up on their own two feet, can be traced directly to Thatcher. Blair himself is not ashamed to admit how much he respects the former prime minister.

As Baroness Thatcher, Margaret Thatcher sits in the House of Lords. She is shown here in her ceremonial robes for the state opening of Parliament.

Even more surprising, the divisions in the **Conservative** party that led to Thatcher's downfall were not resolved after her departure. Although the poll tax was long gone, the split over European **policy** remained. It may erupt at any time and possibly divide the party again.

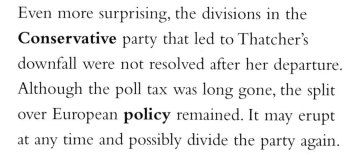

"Like Winston Churchill, she is known for her courage, conviction, determination and willpower. Like Churchill she thrives on **adversity.**"

Inscription on the Winston Churchill Foundation Award, presented to Mrs. Thatcher in Washington, 1988

Margaret Thatcher– Timeline

1925	Margaret Hilda Roberts born in Grantham, Lincolnshire, England (October 13)
1936	Enrolls at Kesteven and Grantham Girls' School
1943	Enters Somerville College, Oxford University
1943	Joins Oxford University Conservative Association (OUCA)
1946	Becomes president of the OUCA
1946	Graduates from Oxford University and takes a job as a research chemist
1950	Loses in election for Member of **Parliament** (M.P.) for the Dartford, Kent, **constituency**
1951	Loses in second attempt to become M.P. for Dartford
1951	Marries Denis Thatcher
1953	Gives birth to twins—Mark and Carol Passes **bar exams** and begins practicing as a lawyer
1959	Elected M.P. for Finchley, north London
1961	Appointed parliamentary secretary at the ministry of pensions
1967	Becomes member of the **shadow cabinet,** in the department of power
1969	Becomes shadow minister for education
1970	Becomes member of the **cabinet** (secretary of state for education and science) when the **Conservatives** gain power
1975	Becomes leader of the Conservative party, succeeding Edward Heath
1979	Leads Conservative party to victory in **general election,** becoming **prime minister**
1982	Leads Britain to victory in Falklands conflict with Argentina

1983	Wins second general election
1984	Survives **IRA** bomb attack at Grand Hotel, Brighton
1985	Defeats Arthur Scargill's **strike** of mineworkers
1987	Wins third general election
1988	Makes famous Bruges speech about Britain's role in Europe
1990	Steps down as party leader and prime minister after Conservative M.P.s vote in leadership contest
1991	Becomes Lady Thatcher of Kesteven and takes seat in the **House of Lords**
1993	Publishes **memoir** of her years in politics
1994	Appointed first woman chancellor of the College of William and Mary in Williamsburg, Virginia
1997	**Labour** party wins control of **House of Commons** for the first time since 1979; Tony Blair becomes prime minister

GLOSSARY

adversity terrible hardship

alderman member of the ruling group of a local council

ally supporter

apartheid former system of South African laws that made it hard for black people to live freely

backbencher M.P. who does not hold a post in the cabinet or shadow cabinet

bar exam exam a person must pass in order to practice law

bill item debated in Parliament, which becomes law if passed

cabinet group of M.P.s chosen by the prime minister to deal with specific aspects of ruling the country

campaign series of planned events to help win an election

candidate someone who runs for office in an election

chancellor of the exchequer cabinet member responsible for running the economy

Cold War period of unfriendly relations between communist and non-communist countries, from 1945 to 1991

compromise when sides each give in a little to solve a problem

condemn to criticize harshly

Conservative political party that believes in low taxes and little government interference in business

constituency area that an M.P. represents in Parliament

councillor in Britain, a person who is elected to a council

currency unit of money that a country uses

democratically by means of democracy—the political system that gives all adults the right to vote

diplomacy solving of problems by discussion rather than by warfare

elite small group of people who have an advantage over others

ennoble to give a special title

European Community (EC) former name of the European Union, a group of European countries with economic and political ties

federal governed by a central body, but allowing areas to keep some powers

foreign secretary government official in charge of international matters

general election election in which the whole country votes for M.P.s and chooses which party will govern

honorary degree degree which recognizes the value of a particular person

hostage person held against his will, usually under threat of death

House of Commons lower house of the British Parliament, where new bills are first debated before becoming law

House of Lords upper house of the British Parliament, where bills are finally debated before becoming law

inflation condition of the economy when prices rise very quickly

Irish Republican Army (IRA) illegal organization that wants to reunite Northern Ireland with the Irish Republic, and which has used terrorism to try to achieve its goal

Labour political party that believes in regulating business and using tax money to help the needy

legislation another name for the process of lawmaking in Parliament

majority number of extra seats the governing party has in Parliament

manifesto plan of action promised by a political party

memoir book of notes, diaries, and recollections

mouthpiece person or group that states the opinions of someone else

NATO North Atlantic Treaty Organization, a military group formed to represent the United States and its allies in the Cold War

opinion poll series of questions asked of the public about their opinions

Opposition political party or parties that do not have a majority in Parliament

Parliament lawmaking body

picket line line of people supporting those workers who are on strike

policy system of political plans

porter someone who carries packages

prime minister leader of the political party that has a majority of seats in Parliament; acts as head of government

privatization selling of companies or property owned by the government to private individuals or companies

prosperous comfortably well-off

public school in Britain, a private school

shadow cabinet group of Opposition M.P.s who are ready to serve if their party is voted into office

share part ownership in a company, which the public can buy

sovereignty accepted right to govern an area or a country

Soviet relating to the Soviet Union

Soviet Union former name of Russia and some of its neighbors

strike to stop work in order to force an employer to give in on disputed issues

superpower either of the two main countries, the United States and the Soviet Union, during the Cold War

task force military weapons and troops sent abroad

tenant someone who rents a house or apartment

term period someone is elected for

terrorist someone who uses illegal violence for a political purpose

thrift care with money

unemployed without work and unable to find another job

union group of people who unite to improve working conditions

United Nations where representatives of all countries discuss world affairs

MORE BOOKS TO READ

Englefield, Dermot, with Janet Seaton and Isobel White. *Facts about the British Prime Ministers: A Compilation of Biographical and Historical Information*. Bronx, N.Y.: H.W. Wilson, 1995.

Hole, Dorothy. *Margaret Thatcher: Britain's Prime Minister*. Berkeley Heights, N.J.: Enslow Publishers, Inc., 1990.

Nardo, Don. *Women Leaders of Nations*. San Diego: Lucent Books, 1998.

INDEX